Chat AI Marketing Mastery: A Practical Guide to Using Chatbots for Your Business

By Tracey Callaghan

CEO iReach Social Media

What it's about

Chat AI Marketing Mastery: A Practical Guide to Using Chatbots for Your Business

Chatbots are rapidly becoming an essential tool for businesses to engage with their customers. With the rise of messaging apps and the increasing demand for instant gratification, businesses need to adapt to stay relevant. Chat AI is an artificial intelligence-based chatbot that can help businesses streamline their customer service, marketing, and sales processes.

In "Chat AI Marketing Mastery," readers will learn how to leverage the power of Chat AI to transform their marketing efforts. The book begins by introducing the concept of chatbots and their relevance in today's business landscape. From there, it delves into the specifics of using Chat AI for marketing, including:

Setting up Chat AI for your business

Creating a conversation flow that reflects your brand and business goals

Leveraging Chat AI to generate leads and sales

Measuring the success of your Chat AI marketing efforts

The book also covers advanced topics such as using Chat AI for customer service, creating personalized experiences for customers, and integrating Chat AI with other marketing tools.

Throughout the book, readers will find practical tips, case studies, and examples of how other businesses have successfully used Chat AI to improve their marketing efforts. By the end of the book, readers will have a solid understanding of how to use Chat AI to create engaging conversations that lead to increased sales and customer satisfaction.

"Chat AI Marketing Mastery" is a must-read for anyone who wants to stay ahead of the curve in the ever-evolving world of marketing. Whether you're a small business owner, a marketer, or a customer service representative, this book will provide you with the knowledge and tools you need to succeed.

Introduction:

In the digital age, customer engagement has become more critical than ever for businesses to thrive. With the rise of messaging apps and the need for instant gratification, chatbots have emerged as a powerful tool for engaging with customers. Chat AI is an advanced chatbot technology that uses artificial intelligence to create engaging conversations with customers.

In "Chat AI Marketing Mastery," readers will learn how to harness the power of Chat AI to revolutionize their marketing strategies. The book begins by introducing the concept of chatbots and their relevance in today's business landscape. It then delves into the specifics of using Chat AI for marketing, including:

Setting up Chat AI for your business

Designing a conversation flow that reflects your brand and business objectives

Utilizing Chat AI to generate leads and sales

Measuring the success of your Chat AI marketing campaigns

The book also covers advanced topics such as integrating Chat AI with other marketing tools, using Chat AI for customer service, and creating personalized experiences for customers.

Throughout the book, readers will find practical tips, case studies, and real-world examples of businesses that have successfully utilized Chat AI to improve their marketing efforts. By the end of the book, readers will have a comprehensive understanding of how to use Chat AI to create engaging conversations that lead to increased sales and customer satisfaction.

"Chat AI Marketing Mastery" is an essential read for anyone who wants to stay ahead of the competition in today's fast-paced digital world. Whether you're a small business owner, a marketer, or a customer service representative, this book provides you with the knowledge and tools you need to succeed in today's ever-evolving market

Chapter 1

Getting Started with Chat AI Marketing

Chatbots have quickly become a go-to tool for businesses looking to engage with their customers in a more efficient and personalized way. Chat AI takes this technology to the next level, utilizing advanced artificial intelligence and machine learning algorithms to create engaging conversations with customers. In this chapter, we'll explore how to get started with Chat AI for your business's marketing efforts.

Step 1: Identify Your Business Goals

Before diving into the world of Chat AI marketing, it's essential to identify your business goals. What do you want to achieve with Chat AI? Do you want to generate leads, increase sales, or improve customer satisfaction? Once you've identified your goals, you can develop a strategy that aligns with them.

Step 2: Choose a Chat AI Provider

Choosing the right Chat AI provider is crucial to the success of your marketing efforts. There are many providers available, each with its strengths and weaknesses. Some popular Chat AI providers include IBM Watson, Google Dialogflow, and Amazon Lex. It's essential to research providers and choose one that aligns with your business goals and budget.

Step 3: Define Your Conversation Flow

The conversation flow is the backbone of your Chat AI marketing strategy. It's essential to design a flow that reflects your brand and business objectives. Consider the types of questions your customers may ask and develop responses that provide value and encourage engagement. Your conversation flow should be dynamic, allowing for natural conversation while guiding customers towards your business objectives.

Step 4: Integrate with Other Marketing Tools

Integrating Chat AI with your other marketing tools can enhance your overall marketing strategy. For example, integrating Chat AI with your email marketing campaign can help you generate more leads and provide a personalized experience for customers.

Step 5: Test and Refine

Testing and refining your Chat AI marketing strategy is essential to its success. Monitor your Chat AI interactions, and gather data on engagement rates, click-through rates, and conversion rates. Use this data to refine your conversation flow, making it more engaging and effective over time.

Conclusion:

Getting started with Chat AI marketing may seem daunting, but with a solid strategy and the right provider, it can be a powerful tool for improving customer engagement and driving business growth. In the following chapters, we'll delve deeper into each step of the process, providing practical tips and real-world examples of businesses that have successfully used Chat AI to transform their marketing efforts.

Chapter 2

Natural Language Processing (NLP) and Chat AI

This chapter will cover the basics of NLP and how it relates to Chat AI. It will cover topics such as:

The different components of NLP (syntax, semantics, and pragmatics) and how they apply to Chat AI

Techniques for extracting meaning from natural language text, such as sentiment analysis and entity recognition

Strategies for improving the accuracy and effectiveness of Chat AI through NLP, such as intent recognition and context awareness

Examples of businesses that have successfully used NLP to improve their Chat AI interactions

Natural Language Processing (NLP) is a field of study that focuses on how computers can understand and interpret human language. It is an essential component of Chat AI because it enables machines to carry on natural and engaging conversations with customers. In this chapter, we will explore the basics of NLP and how it applies to Chat AI.

Section 1: Introduction to Natural Language Processing

NLP is a subfield of artificial intelligence (AI) that deals with the interactions between computers and natural language. It encompasses a wide range of technologies and techniques that enable computers to understand, interpret, and generate human language.

The field of NLP has grown rapidly in recent years, driven by advancements in machine learning and deep learning algorithms. These advancements have enabled computers to process large amounts of natural language data and generate more accurate and useful responses.

NLP is used in a variety of applications, including virtual assistants, chatbots, and automated translation systems. It is also used in customer service, marketing, and other business applications to provide more personalized and engaging interactions with customers.

Section 2: The Components of Natural Language Processing

NLP consists of three main components: syntax, semantics, and pragmatics. These components work together to enable computers to understand and interpret human language.

Syntax refers to the structure and rules of language. It deals with how words are combined to form sentences and how sentences are structured to convey meaning. Syntax is important in NLP because it enables computers to identify the grammatical structure of sentences and understand how they relate to each other.

Semantics refers to the meaning of language. It deals with how words and sentences convey meaning and how that meaning is interpreted by humans. Semantics is important in NLP because it enables computers to understand the meaning of natural language text and generate responses that are contextually appropriate.

Pragmatics refers to the social and cultural aspects of language. It deals with how language is used in different contexts and how it is interpreted by different people. Pragmatics is important in NLP because it enables computers to understand the social and cultural context of language and generate responses that are appropriate for a given situation.

Section 3: Techniques for Extracting Meaning from Natural Language Text

One of the primary goals of NLP is to extract meaning from natural language text. There are several techniques that are commonly used for this purpose, including sentiment analysis, entity recognition, and topic modelling.

Sentiment analysis is a technique for determining the sentiment or emotion expressed in a piece of text. It is commonly used in social media monitoring and customer service applications to gauge customer sentiment and identify potential issues.

Entity recognition is a technique for identifying and extracting named entities from a piece of text. Named entities can include people, places, organizations, and other specific entities that are mentioned in the text. Entity recognition is important in NLP because it enables computers to understand the context of a piece of text and generate more accurate and relevant responses.

Topic modelling is a technique for identifying the main topics or themes in a piece of text. It is commonly used in applications such as news aggregation and content analysis to identify key topics and trends in large amounts of text data.

Section 4: Improving Chat AI with NLP

NLP is essential for developing Chat AI that can carry on natural and engaging conversations with customers. There are several strategies that can be used to improve Chat AI with NLP, including intent recognition and context awareness.

Intent recognition is a technique for identifying the intent behind a customer's request or question. It is important in Chat AI because it enables computers to generate more relevant and useful responses based on the customer's intent

Chapter 3: Machine Learning and Chat AI

In this chapter, we'll explore the role of machine learning in Chat AI. The chapter will cover:

The basics of machine learning, including supervised and unsupervised learning

The different types of machine learning algorithms commonly used in Chat AI, such as decision trees and neural networks

The use of reinforcement learning to train Chat AI to learn from experience and improve its interactions with customers

Best practices for incorporating machine learning into Chat AI development, such as selecting the right training data and monitoring the performance of the model

Case studies of companies that have successfully implemented machine learning in their Chat AI strategies

Machine learning is a subset of artificial intelligence that involves training computer algorithms to identify patterns in data and make decisions based on those patterns. Machine learning is a key component of Chat AI because it enables machines to learn from customer interactions and improve their responses over time. In this chapter, we will explore the basics of machine learning and how it applies to Chat AI.

Section 1: Introduction to Machine Learning

Machine learning is a type of artificial intelligence that involves training computer algorithms to identify patterns in data and make decisions based on those patterns. It is used in a variety of applications, including natural language processing, computer vision, and predictive analytics.

Machine learning algorithms can be categorized into three main types: supervised learning, unsupervised learning, and reinforcement learning. Supervised learning involves training a machine learning model on a labelled dataset, while unsupervised learning involves training a model on an unlabelled dataset. Reinforcement learning involves training a model to make decisions based on feedback from the environment.

Section 2: Machine Learning Techniques for Chat AI

Machine learning is a key component of Chat AI because it enables machines to learn from customer interactions and improve their responses over time. There are several machine learning techniques that are commonly used in Chat AI, including natural language processing, deep learning, and decision trees.

Natural language processing (NLP) is a subset of machine learning that deals with the interactions between computers and human language. It is used in Chat AI to enable machines to understand and interpret natural language text and generate responses that are contextually appropriate.

Deep learning is a type of machine learning that involves training neural networks to learn from large amounts of data. It is used in Chat AI to enable machines to identify patterns in customer interactions and improve their responses over time.

Decision trees are a type of machine learning algorithm that involves building a tree-like model of decisions and their possible consequences. They are commonly used in Chat AI to help machines make decisions based on the customer's input and previous interactions.

Section 3: Training Chat AI with Machine Learning

Training Chat AI with machine learning involves collecting and labelling data, building and training machine learning models, and evaluating the performance of those models. There are several strategies that can be used to improve the performance of Chat AI with machine learning, including data augmentation, hyperparameter tuning, and transfer learning.

Data augmentation involves generating additional data from the existing dataset to improve the performance of the machine learning model. This can include techniques such as adding noise to the data, rotating images, or translating text.

Hyperparameter tuning involves adjusting the parameters of the machine learning model to improve its performance. This can include techniques such as adjusting the learning rate, the number of hidden layers in a neural network, or the number of decision trees in a random forest.

Transfer learning involves using a pre-trained machine learning model as the basis for a new model. This can be useful in Chat AI because it enables machines to learn from a large amount of data without requiring a large amount of new data to be labelled and collected.

Section 4: The Future of Machine Learning and Chat AI

The future of machine learning and Chat AI is bright, with many new advancements and innovations on the horizon. Some of the key trends to watch in the coming years include the integration of machine learning with other AI technologies, such as computer vision and natural language processing, the development of more advanced deep learning techniques, and the use of machine learning to create more personalized and engaging customer experiences.

One of the most promising areas of development in Chat AI is the use of reinforcement learning to create more interactive and engaging chatbots. Reinforcement learning involves training a machine learning model to make decisions based on feedback from the environment, which can enable chatbots to learn from user interactions and adapt their responses to provide a more personalized and engaging experience. This can be particularly useful in applications such as customer service, where chatbots can learn from previous interactions to provide more efficient and effective support.

Another area of development in Chat AI is the integration of machine learning with natural language processing and computer vision. This can enable chatbots to understand not only text but also visual cues such as facial expressions and body language, which can provide a more nuanced understanding of the user's needs and preferences. This can lead to more effective communication and a more personalized experience for the user.

In addition, advancements in deep learning techniques are expected to drive further innovation in Chat AI. Deep learning involves training neural networks with large amounts of data to identify complex patterns and relationships. This can enable chatbots to understand more complex language and provide more accurate and helpful responses to user queries.

Finally, machine learning is expected to play an increasingly important role in creating personalized and engaging customer experiences. By analysing customer data and preferences, chatbots can adapt their responses to provide a more personalized experience for each individual user. This can lead to increased customer satisfaction and loyalty, as well as improved business outcomes such as increased sales and customer retention.

In conclusion, machine learning is a key component of Chat AI, enabling machines to learn from customer interactions and improve their responses over time. By leveraging machine learning techniques such as natural language processing, deep learning, and decision trees, chatbots can provide more accurate, personalized, and engaging customer experiences. As advancements in machine learning continue to drive innovation in Chat AI, we can expect to see even more exciting developments and applications in the years to come.

Chapter 3

Best Practices for Using Chat AI in Marketing

Chat AI is a powerful tool for businesses looking to improve their marketing efforts. By enabling personalized interactions with customers, chatbots can help businesses build stronger relationships with their audience and drive more conversions. However, to get the most out of Chat AI, it's important to follow best practices that ensure your chatbot is effective, efficient, and engaging. In this chapter, we'll explore some key best practices for using Chat AI in marketing.

Define Your Goals

Before you start building your chatbot, it's important to define your goals. What do you hope to achieve with your chatbot? Do you want to drive more leads, improve customer satisfaction, or increase sales? Defining your goals will help you determine the features and functionality you need to include in your chatbot, as well as the metrics you'll use to measure success.

Identify Your Target Audience

To create an effective chatbot, you need to understand your target audience. Who are they? What are their pain points and challenges? What questions do they typically ask? By understanding your audience, you can tailor your chatbot's responses to their specific needs, providing a more personalized experience that will resonate with them.

Choose the Right Platform

There are many different platforms available for building chatbots, each with its own strengths and weaknesses. Some popular options include Facebook Messenger, WhatsApp, and Slack. When choosing a platform, consider factors such as your target audience, the functionality you need, and the ease of integration with your existing systems.

Use Natural Language Processing

One of the key benefits of Chat AI is the ability to understand and respond to natural language. To make the most of this capability, it's important to use natural language processing (NLP) to build your chatbot. NLP enables your chatbot to understand the nuances of human language, allowing it to provide more accurate and helpful responses to user queries.

Personalize Your Interactions

Personalization is key to creating engaging and effective chatbot interactions. By leveraging user data such as past purchases or browsing history, you can tailor your chatbot's responses to each individual user. This can help build stronger relationships with your audience and drive more conversions.

Test and Iterate

Like any marketing tool, Chat AI requires testing and iteration to ensure it's effective. Before launching your chatbot, it's important to test it thoroughly to identify any issues or areas for improvement. Once your chatbot is live, continue to monitor its performance and make tweaks as needed to ensure it's delivering the results you want.

Provide Clear Next Steps

Finally, it's important to provide clear next steps for users interacting with your chatbot. Whether it's directing them to a specific page on your website or encouraging them to sign up for a newsletter, providing clear next steps can help ensure your chatbot is driving conversions and achieving your marketing goals.

In conclusion, Chat AI can be a powerful tool for businesses looking to improve their marketing efforts. By following best practices such as defining your goals, identifying your target audience, choosing the right platform, using natural language processing, personalizing your interactions, testing and iterating, and providing clear next steps, you can build an effective and engaging chatbot that delivers results. As advancements in Chat AI continue to drive innovation in the field, we can expect even more exciting applications and opportunities for businesses to leverage this powerful technology.

Chapter 4

Common Pitfalls to Avoid When Using Chat AI in Marketing

While Chat AI can be a valuable asset in your marketing strategy, there are some common pitfalls that businesses can fall into if they're not careful. By understanding these pitfalls and learning how to avoid them, you can ensure your chatbot is effective and engaging, delivering results that help drive your marketing goals forward. In this chapter, we'll explore some common pitfalls to avoid when using Chat AI in marketing.

Overreliance on Automation

While Chat AI is designed to automate many customer interactions, it's important to strike a balance between automation and human touch. Overreliance on automation can make your chatbot feel impersonal and robotic, which can turn users off and even hurt your brand reputation. Be sure to include human touchpoints where appropriate, such as providing a live chat option or directing users to a customer support representative.

Lack of Personalization

Personalization is key to creating engaging and effective chatbot interactions. However, if your chatbot doesn't have access to user data or if it's not properly integrated with your systems, it can be difficult to deliver personalized experiences to your audience. Make sure you have a strategy in place for collecting and leveraging user data to personalize your interactions.

Failure to Understand Your Audience

In order to create a chatbot that resonates with your audience, you need to understand their needs, pain points, and preferences. Failure to understand your audience can result in a chatbot that misses the mark and fails to engage users. Conduct market research and customer surveys to gain a better understanding of your audience and their needs.

Lack of Testing and Iteration

Testing and iteration are critical to the success of your chatbot. Without testing, you won't know whether your chatbot is effective or where it needs improvement. Without iteration, you won't be able to make the changes necessary to optimize your chatbot for success. Make sure you have a plan in place for testing and iterating your chatbot regularly.

Poor Integration with Existing Systems

Your chatbot needs to be properly integrated with your existing systems in order to be effective. Without integration, your chatbot may not be able to access the data it needs to deliver personalized experiences, or it may not be able to trigger the actions necessary to drive conversions. Make sure you work closely with your IT department or chatbot provider to ensure proper integration.

Lack of Clear Next Steps

Your chatbot should always provide clear next steps for users. Whether it's directing them to a specific page on your website or encouraging them to sign up for a newsletter, providing clear next steps can help ensure your chatbot is driving conversions and achieving your marketing goals. Make sure your chatbot is designed with clear next steps in mind.

In conclusion, while Chat AI can be a powerful tool for businesses looking to improve their marketing efforts, it's important to be aware of common pitfalls and take steps to avoid them. By avoiding overreliance on automation, prioritizing personalization, understanding your audience, testing and iterating regularly, ensuring proper integration with existing systems, and providing clear next steps, you can create a chatbot that delivers results and helps drive your marketing goals forward. By being thoughtful and intentional in your approach, you can leverage the power of Chat AI to build stronger relationships with your audience and drive more conversions.

Chapter 5

Using Chat AI for social media

Social media has become an integral part of our daily lives, with billions of people around the world using it to connect with friends and family, follow their favourite brands, and discover new products and services. With the rise of chat AI, businesses have a powerful tool at their disposal to engage with users on social media platforms, delivering personalized experiences that can help drive conversions and build brand loyalty.

There are several reasons why businesses should consider using chat AI in social media marketing:

Instant Engagement

Social media platforms are designed to encourage instant engagement, with users able to quickly and easily like, comment, and share content they find interesting. By incorporating chat AI into your social media strategy, you can provide users with instant engagement opportunities that keep them coming back for more. Chat AI can be used to deliver personalized messages, answer questions, and provide helpful recommendations, all in real-time.

Personalization

Personalization is key to creating engaging social media experiences that resonate with users. Chat AI can help deliver personalized experiences by analysing user data and delivering content that is relevant to their interests, preferences, and past behaviour. By delivering personalized experiences, businesses can build stronger relationships with their audience and increase the likelihood of conversions.

Cost-Effective

Chat AI can be a cost-effective way to engage with users on social media platforms. While traditional methods of social media marketing often require significant resources, such as time and personnel, chat AI can automate many of these processes, saving businesses time and money. By automating certain interactions, chat AI can help businesses scale their social media efforts more efficiently, reaching more users and driving more conversions.

24/7 Availability

One of the key advantages of chat AI is its 24/7 availability. While businesses may not have the resources to respond to user inquiries around the clock, chat AI can provide instant responses at any time of day or night. This can help improve user satisfaction and increase conversions by providing users with the information they need when they need it.

Improved User Experience

At the heart of social media marketing is the user experience. By using chat AI to provide personalized, engaging experiences, businesses can improve the user experience and build stronger relationships with their audience. Chat AI can help businesses provide faster, more accurate responses to user inquiries, and can even anticipate user needs before they arise, delivering a seamless experience that keeps users coming back for more.

In conclusion, using chat AI in social media marketing can be a powerful way to engage with users, build stronger relationships, and drive conversions. By delivering personalized experiences, automating certain processes, and providing instant responses 24/7, businesses can improve the user experience and drive results on social media platforms. As social media continues to play an important role in our daily lives, businesses that leverage the power of chat AI will be well-positioned to succeed in today's fast-paced digital landscape.

Chapter 6

Can Chat AI help you to improve your website SEO?

Search Engine Optimization (SEO) is a critical component of any successful digital marketing strategy. It involves optimizing your website to rank higher in search engine results pages, driving more traffic to your site and increasing the likelihood of conversions. While traditional SEO strategies focus on optimizing website content and structure, chat AI can be a powerful tool to enhance your website's SEO efforts. In this chapter, we'll explore how chat AI can help improve your website's SEO.

Improved User Engagement

User engagement is a crucial factor in website SEO. The more engaged users are with your website, the longer they will stay, and the higher the chances they will convert. Chat AI can be used to enhance user engagement by providing personalized experiences that cater to the user's needs and preferences. By analysing user data, chat AI can deliver content that is relevant and engaging, increasing the likelihood that users will stay on your site and interact with your content.

Improved Site Navigation

Site navigation is a critical factor in website SEO. Search engines reward websites that have easy-to-use navigation and penalize those that have complicated or confusing navigation. Chat AI can help improve site navigation by providing users with instant access to the information they need. By analysing user behaviour, chat AI can anticipate user needs and deliver content that is relevant and easy to find, improving the user experience and increasing the likelihood of conversions.

Enhanced Keyword Research

Keyword research is a critical component of website SEO. It involves identifying the most relevant and valuable keywords for your website and using them strategically throughout your content. Chat AI can be used to enhance keyword research by analysing user data and identifying the most popular search terms related to your business. By using these insights to inform your keyword strategy, you can improve your website's visibility in search engine results pages, driving more traffic to your site.

Improved Content Optimization

Content optimization is a key aspect of website SEO. It involves optimizing your website's content to ensure it is relevant, valuable, and engaging for your target audience. Chat AI can be used to improve content optimization by analysing user behaviour and delivering content that is tailored to the user's needs and preferences. By providing personalized experiences, chat AI can improve user engagement and increase the likelihood of conversions, driving more traffic to your site and improving your website's SEO.

Improved User Experience

At the heart of website SEO is the user experience. Search engines reward websites that provide a positive user experience, and penalize those that provide a poor one. Chat AI can help improve the user experience by providing personalized experiences that cater to the user's needs and preferences. By analysing user data and delivering content that is relevant and engaging, chat AI can improve user engagement, increase the likelihood of conversions, and improve your website's SEO.

In conclusion, chat AI can be a powerful tool to improve your website's SEO efforts. By providing personalized experiences, improving site navigation, enhancing keyword research, optimizing content, and improving the user experience, chat AI can help drive more traffic to your site, increase user engagement, and improve the likelihood of conversions. As SEO continues to play a critical role in digital marketing, businesses that leverage the power of chat AI will be well-positioned to succeed in today's competitive online landscape.

Chapter 7

Boost Your Email Marketing Strategy with Chat AI

Email marketing remains a critical component of any successful digital marketing strategy. It allows businesses to reach out to their audience directly, build relationships, and drive conversions. However, with increasing competition and changing consumer behaviour, email marketing is becoming more challenging than ever. This is where Chat AI comes in. By leveraging the power of artificial intelligence and chatbots, businesses can enhance their email marketing efforts and improve their chances of success. In this article, we'll explore how Chat AI can help you with your email marketing strategy and provide tips on how to get started.

Personalization

Personalization is a key aspect of effective email marketing. By tailoring emails to the recipient's interests and preferences, businesses can increase engagement and drive conversions. However, manually personalizing emails can be time-consuming and challenging, especially for businesses with large email lists. Chat AI can help automate the personalization process by analysing user data and delivering personalized content to each recipient. By using chatbots to deliver personalized content, businesses can improve engagement and increase conversions.

Segmentation

Segmentation is another critical aspect of effective email marketing. By dividing your email list into smaller groups based on demographics, interests, and behaviours, businesses can tailor their emails to each group's unique needs and preferences. However, manually segmenting email lists can be time-consuming and challenging, especially for businesses with large email lists. Chat AI can help automate the segmentation process by analysing user data and segmenting email lists based on user behaviour. By using chatbots to segment email lists, businesses can improve engagement and increase conversions.

Lead Generation

Lead generation is a crucial aspect of email marketing. It involves capturing the contact information of potential customers and nurturing them into paying customers. Chat AI can help improve lead generation efforts by using chatbots to capture contact information and provide personalized content to potential customers. By automating lead generation, businesses can save time and resources while improving the effectiveness of their email marketing campaigns.

Behavioural Targeting

Behavioural targeting is a powerful technique that involves analysing user behaviour to deliver targeted content. By analysing user behaviour, businesses can tailor their emails to each recipient's unique needs and preferences, increasing engagement and driving conversions. Chat AI can help automate the behavioural targeting process by analysing user data and delivering targeted content to each recipient. By using chatbots to deliver targeted content, businesses can improve engagement and increase conversions.

A/B Testing

A/B testing is a critical aspect of effective email marketing. It involves testing different versions of emails to determine which performs best. By testing different versions of emails, businesses can identify the most effective subject lines, content, and calls to action, improving the effectiveness of their email marketing campaigns. Chat AI can help automate the A/B testing process by analysing user data and delivering different versions of emails to each recipient. By using chatbots to deliver different versions of emails, businesses can save time and resources while improving the effectiveness of their email marketing campaigns.

In conclusion, Chat AI can be a powerful tool to enhance your email marketing strategy. By leveraging the power of artificial intelligence and chatbots, businesses can improve personalization, segmentation, lead generation, behavioural targeting, and A/B testing efforts, driving more engagement and conversions. As email marketing continues to evolve, businesses that embrace the power of Chat AI will be well-positioned to succeed in today's competitive online landscape.

Chapter 8

Get the research done on Chat AI

Marketing research is a critical aspect of any successful marketing strategy. It involves gathering data on your target audience, analysing the data, and using the insights to make informed marketing decisions. Chat AI can be a powerful tool for conducting marketing research, as it can provide businesses with real-time data and insights into customer behaviour and preferences. Here are some ways in which businesses can use chat AI to conduct marketing research:

Chatbots for Surveys

One of the most common ways to gather data on your target audience is through surveys. However, conducting surveys manually can be time-consuming and resource-intensive. Chatbots can help automate the survey process by delivering surveys directly to customers and collecting responses in real-time. By using chatbots for surveys, businesses can gather data on customer preferences, behaviours, and attitudes, and use the insights to improve their marketing strategy.

Sentiment Analysis

Sentiment analysis involves analysing customer feedback to understand their emotions and opinions. By analysing customer sentiment, businesses can gain insights into customer satisfaction, identify potential issues, and make informed marketing decisions. Chat AI can help automate the sentiment analysis process by using natural language processing to analyse customer feedback and provide insights into customer sentiment. By using sentiment analysis, businesses can make data-driven decisions and improve their marketing strategy.

Behavioural Analysis

Behavioural analysis involves analysing customer behaviour to understand their preferences and needs. By analysing customer behaviour, businesses can gain insights into customer preferences, identify potential issues, and make informed marketing decisions. Chat AI can help automate the behavioural analysis process by tracking customer interactions with chatbots and analysing the data to provide insights into customer behaviour. By using behavioural analysis, businesses can make data-driven decisions and improve their marketing strategy.

Real-time Analytics

Real-time analytics involve analysing customer data in real-time to gain insights into customer behaviour and preferences. By using chatbots to deliver personalized content and track customer interactions, businesses can gather real-time data on customer behaviour and use the insights to improve their marketing strategy. Chat AI can help automate the real-time analytics process by analysing customer data in real-time and providing insights into customer behaviour and preferences. By using real-time analytics, businesses can make data-driven decisions and improve their marketing strategy.

Chat AI can be a powerful tool for conducting marketing research. By using chatbots for surveys, sentiment analysis, behavioural analysis, and real-time analytics, businesses can gather real-time data and insights into customer behaviour and preferences. By using the insights gained through chat AI, businesses can make data-driven decisions and improve their marketing strategy, ultimately leading to increased engagement and conversions.

Chapter 9

Beyond FAQs: How Chat AI Can Revolutionize Your Customer Service

In today's fast-paced business environment, customers expect quick and personalized support when they have questions or issues. Traditional customer service channels such as email and phone support can be slow and impersonal, leading to frustration and dissatisfaction among customers. This is where chat AI can make a significant impact. By leveraging the power of machine learning and natural language processing, chat AI can provide personalized and efficient customer support to meet the needs and expectations of today's customers.

In this chapter, we'll explore how chat AI can revolutionize your customer service strategy by offering personalized support, resolving issues, and answering common questions. We'll discuss the benefits of using chat AI for customer service and provide practical tips on how to implement this technology in your business.

Personalized Support with Chat AI

One of the key advantages of using chat AI for customer service is the ability to provide personalized support to customers. With chat AI, businesses can collect data on customer behaviour, preferences, and past interactions to deliver personalized recommendations and support. For example, if a customer has previously purchased a certain product, chat AI can suggest complementary products or offer personalized promotions based on their previous purchase behaviour.

Chat AI can also offer personalized support by leveraging natural language processing (NLP) technology. With NLP, chat AI can understand customer inquiries and respond with relevant answers, without the need for customers to navigate through a complex phone tree or wait for a response from an email ticket system.

Resolving Issues with Chat AI

Another key benefit of chat AI for customer service is the ability to resolve issues quickly and efficiently. Chat AI can handle simple customer inquiries and provide immediate answers, freeing up customer service representatives to focus on more complex issues that require human intervention.

Moreover, chat AI can also provide intelligent routing, which means that customer inquiries are routed to the right department or representative based on the nature of the inquiry. This ensures that customers receive the appropriate support they need and reduces the chance of issues being escalated or unresolved.

Answering Common Questions with Chat AI

One of the most common use cases for chat AI in customer service is answering common questions. Frequently Asked Questions (FAQs) can be easily programmed into chat AI, allowing customers to quickly find answers to their inquiries. This can significantly reduce the volume of inquiries that need to be handled by human representatives, allowing them to focus on more complex issues.

Furthermore, chat AI can also learn from previous customer inquiries and improve its responses over time. By analysing customer behaviour and feedback, chat AI can continuously refine its responses to provide more accurate and relevant answers to customer inquiries.

Practical Tips for Implementing Chat AI in Customer Service

Implementing chat AI in your customer service strategy can be a daunting task. Here are some practical tips to help you get started:

Identify areas of your customer service strategy that can be automated with chat AI, such as FAQs or simple inquiries.

Choose a chat AI platform that aligns with your business needs and offers the features you require, such as natural language processing and intelligent routing.

Train your chat AI platform with accurate and up-to-date data to ensure it provides accurate and relevant answers to customer inquiries.

Integrate chat AI with your existing customer service channels to ensure a seamless experience for customers.

Monitor chat AI interactions and customer feedback to continuously refine and improve your chat AI strategy.

Conclusion

Chat AI offers significant benefits for businesses looking to revolutionize their customer service strategy. By providing personalized support, resolving issues quickly and efficiently, and answering common questions, chat AI can improve the customer experience and reduce the workload of customer service representatives. By following practical tips for implementing chat AI, businesses can leverage this technology to meet the needs and expectations of today's customers.

Chapter 10

Revolutionise Your Lead Generation Strategy with Chat AI

businesses must be innovative in their approach to generate leads. The traditional methods of cold calling and email blasts are becoming less effective, and customers expect personalized experiences. This is where Chat AI comes in - it can revolutionize your lead generation strategy by delivering personalized content to potential customers and tracking their interactions to identify potential leads. In this chapter, we'll explore how Chat AI can be used to generate leads and help businesses reach their goals.

Chat AI allows businesses to engage with potential customers in a more personalized and interactive way. Instead of sending out generic email blasts, Chat AI can be used to deliver personalized content to potential customers based on their preferences and behaviours. By using Chat AI, businesses can provide valuable information to potential customers, which will help build trust and establish credibility.

One of the most significant advantages of Chat AI is its ability to track customer interactions. By analysing these interactions, businesses can identify potential leads and tailor their marketing strategies accordingly. For example, if a potential customer repeatedly asks about a particular product or service, businesses can offer more information or even a personalized demo to convert them into a lead.

Chat AI can also be used to qualify leads. By using chatbots to ask qualifying questions, businesses can identify potential leads and prioritize them accordingly. This can help businesses save time and resources by focusing on the most promising leads.

Another advantage of Chat AI is its ability to integrate with other marketing channels. For example, businesses can use Chat AI to engage with potential customers on social media or even on their website. By integrating Chat AI with other channels, businesses can create a seamless and consistent customer experience across all touchpoints.

To make the most of Chat AI for lead generation, businesses need to develop a comprehensive strategy. This includes setting clear goals, identifying target audiences, and creating a content plan that aligns with their marketing objectives. Additionally, businesses need to ensure that their Chat AI solution is optimized for lead generation and provides relevant information to potential customers.

In conclusion, Chat AI can be a game-changer for businesses looking to generate leads and boost their sales. By delivering personalized content, tracking customer interactions, and integrating with other marketing channels, businesses can create a seamless and engaging customer experience that leads to increased leads

Chapter 11

The Future of Chat AI in Marketing

Chat AI is rapidly becoming a popular tool for businesses looking to engage with their customers and drive conversions. From lead generation to customer support, Chat AI has the potential to transform the way businesses operate. However, the future of Chat AI is even more exciting, with new advancements and innovations that are set to take the technology to new heights. In this chapter, we'll explore the future of Chat AI in marketing and what businesses can expect in the years to come.

One of the most significant advancements in Chat AI is its ability to understand natural language processing (NLP). NLP allows Chat AI to better understand the context of customer inquiries and provide more accurate responses. With the increasing demand for personalized experiences, NLP will be a critical component of Chat AI in the future. Businesses will be able to use NLP-powered Chat AI to understand customer intent, recommend products or services, and provide tailored support.

Another area where Chat AI is set to evolve is through the use of machine learning. Machine learning algorithms enable Chat AI to learn from previous interactions with customers and continuously improve its responses. This will make Chat AI even more intelligent and responsive, helping businesses to better understand their customers' needs and provide more personalized experiences.

Chat AI is also set to become more proactive in its interactions with customers. Instead of waiting for customers to initiate a conversation, Chat AI will be able to anticipate their needs and provide relevant information in real-time. This could include product recommendations, promotions, or even personalized content. By being more proactive, Chat AI will help businesses to create a more engaging and satisfying customer experience.

Finally, Chat AI is set to become more ubiquitous in its deployment. With advancements in chatbot development platforms, businesses of all sizes will be able to create and deploy Chat AI solutions quickly and easily. This will help to democratize the technology and make it more accessible to businesses that may not have the resources to develop their own Chat AI solutions.

In conclusion, the future of Chat AI in marketing is exciting and full of potential. With advancements in NLP, machine learning, proactive interactions, and more accessible deployment, Chat AI will continue to transform the way businesses engage with their customers. As businesses look to stay competitive in an increasingly digital world, Chat AI will become an essential tool for success. It's time to embrace the future of Chat AI and take advantage of all that it has to offer.

Chapter 12

Closing the Deal: How Chat AI Can Boost Your Sales Strategy

As businesses look to improve their sales strategy and increase revenue, Chat AI has emerged as a powerful tool to engage with potential customers and close more deals. In this chapter, we'll explore how Chat AI can help businesses deliver personalized sales pitches, track interactions, and identify potential leads to close more deals.

One of the most significant advantages of Chat AI in sales is its ability to deliver personalized sales pitches. By analysing customer data and behaviour, Chat AI can provide tailored product recommendations and promotional offers that resonate with potential customers. This personalized approach helps to build trust and increase the likelihood of a sale. Chat AI can also be used to answer any questions or concerns that potential customers may have in real-time, helping to alleviate any doubts they may have about the product or service.

Another way Chat AI can boost your sales strategy is by tracking interactions with potential customers. By collecting data on customer behaviour and preferences, businesses can gain insights into what works and what doesn't in their sales strategy. This data can be used to improve sales pitches, target specific customer segments, and optimize the overall sales process. By tracking interactions with potential customers, Chat AI can also identify potential leads and flag them for sales teams to follow up with, ensuring that no potential opportunities slip through the cracks.

Chat AI can also assist in closing deals by providing additional support during the sales process. This could include offering discounts, product demos, or even personalized video presentations. By providing these additional resources, Chat AI can help to push potential customers towards making a purchase and increase the likelihood of a successful sale.

Finally, Chat AI can improve the efficiency of the sales process by automating repetitive tasks and freeing up sales teams to focus on closing deals. For example, Chat AI can handle basic customer inquiries and scheduling appointments, allowing sales teams to focus on building relationships and closing deals.

In conclusion, Chat AI can be a valuable tool for businesses looking to improve their sales strategy and close more deals. By delivering personalized sales pitches, tracking interactions, identifying potential leads, and providing additional support during the sales process, Chat AI can help businesses to build trust with potential customers and increase the likelihood of a successful sale. With the help of Chat AI, businesses can streamline their sales process and focus on what really matters - closing deals and driving revenue.

Chapter 13

Powering Up Your Chat AI: Effective Prompts to Boost Your Marketing

Chat AI has become an essential tool for businesses looking to improve their marketing strategy and engage with customers in real-time. However, the effectiveness of Chat AI depends on the quality of its prompts. In this chapter, we'll explore how effective prompts can be used to boost your marketing efforts and maximize the potential of Chat AI.

First, let's define what we mean by prompts in Chat AI. A prompt is a pre-written message or question that Chat AI uses to engage with customers. Prompts can be customized to fit different customer segments and marketing goals. Effective prompts should be engaging, relevant, and personalized to maximize their impact.

One of the most effective ways to use prompts in Chat AI is to engage customers with personalized questions. By asking questions about their interests and preferences, businesses can tailor their marketing efforts to match customer needs. For example, a clothing retailer might ask a customer about their style preferences or favourite colours to recommend personalized outfit options. This personalized approach helps to build trust with customers and increase the likelihood of a purchase.

Another effective prompt strategy is to use chat AI to initiate conversations with customers proactively. This could include offering promotional discounts, sharing personalized content, or simply greeting customers and inviting them to engage with the business. By being proactive, businesses can engage with customers who may not have reached out on their own and provide added value that increases the likelihood of a purchase.

Chat AI can also be used to provide personalized product recommendations based on customer behaviour and preferences. For example, an e-commerce store might suggest complementary products or related items based on a customer's purchase history. These personalized recommendations can help customers discover new products and increase the likelihood of a repeat purchase.

Finally, prompts can be used to collect feedback from customers and improve the overall customer experience. For example, businesses can use Chat AI to ask customers for feedback on their recent purchase or interaction with the business. This feedback can be used to identify areas for improvement and tailor marketing efforts to better meet customer needs.

In conclusion, effective prompts are a critical component of Chat AI's marketing strategy. By engaging customers with personalized questions, initiating conversations proactively, providing personalized recommendations, and collecting feedback, businesses can use Chat AI to build trust, increase customer engagement, and ultimately drive revenue. With the right prompts in place, Chat AI can be a powerful tool for businesses looking to improve their marketing efforts and stay ahead of the competition.

Chapter 14

Amplifying Your Brand with Chat AI: Crafting Taglines and Branding Messages

In the world of marketing, a strong brand is essential for standing out in a crowded marketplace. Branding is more than just creating a logo and slapping it on everything; it's about creating a unique identity that resonates with your target audience. In this chapter, we'll explore how Chat AI can help you craft taglines and branding messages that capture your brand's essence and resonate with your customers.

Chat AI can assist in crafting the perfect tagline or slogan that represents your brand. With its natural language processing capabilities, Chat AI can analyse your brand's tone and voice to create a tagline that encapsulates the essence of your brand. Chat AI can even test multiple tagline options to see which one resonates best with your target audience. With Chat AI's help, you can create a memorable and effective tagline that sets your brand apart.

Chat AI can also assist with crafting branding messages that are consistent across all of your marketing channels. By analysing your brand's tone and voice, Chat AI can create messaging that's in line with your brand's identity. Chat AI can also help with testing different messaging options to see which ones resonate with your audience. By utilizing Chat AI, you can ensure that your brand messaging is consistent and effective across all channels.

Another way Chat AI can help with branding is by identifying brand mentions and sentiment in customer conversations. By tracking conversations across different channels, Chat AI can identify how your brand is perceived and identify areas where your brand messaging needs improvement. This information can be used to adjust branding messages and improve customer perception of your brand.

In conclusion, Chat AI can help businesses create strong branding by crafting effective taglines and consistent messaging across all marketing channels. Chat AI can also assist with tracking brand mentions and sentiment to identify areas for improvement. With Chat AI's help, businesses can amplify their brand and stand out in a crowded marketplace.

Chapter 15

Powering Your Hashtag Strategy with Chat AI: Finding the Right Hashtags for Your Business

Hashtags are a powerful tool for businesses to reach a wider audience and increase their social media presence. However, selecting the right hashtags can be a challenging task. In this chapter, we'll explore how Chat AI can help businesses select the right hashtags to improve their social media presence and reach.

Chat AI can assist in identifying relevant hashtags based on the content of the post. By analysing the text and context of the post, Chat AI can suggest hashtags that are relevant to the content. This can save time and effort in selecting the right hashtags and ensure that the post is reaching the right audience.

Chat AI can also help with analysing hashtag performance. By tracking the performance of hashtags over time, Chat AI can identify which hashtags are performing well and which ones are not. This information can be used to adjust the hashtag strategy and improve social media performance.

Another way Chat AI can assist with selecting the right hashtags is by analysing competitor hashtags. By analysing the hashtags used by competitors, Chat AI can identify which ones are performing well and suggest similar hashtags for the business to use. This can help businesses stay competitive and reach a wider audience.

Chat AI can also help with monitoring hashtags. By monitoring the performance of specific hashtags, Chat AI can identify trending topics and adjust the content strategy to include these topics. This can help businesses stay relevant and improve social media engagement.

In conclusion, Chat AI can help businesses select the right hashtags by suggesting relevant hashtags based on the content of the post, analysing hashtag performance, analysing competitor hashtags, and monitoring hashtags. With Chat AI's help, businesses can improve their social media presence and reach a wider audience.

Chapter 16

Streamlining Your Marketing Reports with Chat AI

Marketing reports are an essential part of any business's marketing strategy. However, they can be time-consuming and tedious to create. In this chapter, we'll explore how Chat AI can help streamline the marketing report process and provide valuable insights.

Chat AI can assist with data analysis, making it easier to generate marketing reports. By analysing data from various sources, Chat AI can identify patterns and trends that are relevant to the business. This information can be used to create reports that provide valuable insights into the business's marketing performance.

Chat AI can also help with report customization. By analysing the business's marketing goals and objectives, Chat AI can suggest relevant metrics and data points to include in the report. This can save time and effort in creating customized reports that are tailored to the business's needs.

Another way Chat AI can assist with marketing reports is by providing real-time updates. By tracking data in real-time, Chat AI can provide updates on marketing performance, allowing businesses to make adjustments and stay on track with their marketing goals.

Chat AI can also help with report visualization. By creating visually appealing reports, businesses can better communicate their marketing performance to stakeholders. Chat AI can assist with creating charts, graphs, and other visual aids that make it easier to understand complex data.

In conclusion, Chat AI can help streamline the marketing report process by assisting with data analysis, report customization, providing real-time updates, and report visualization. With Chat AI's help, businesses can create reports that provide valuable insights and improve their marketing performance.